Discover

How to Know God and Do His Will

Jay Simala

Discover: How to Know God and Do His Will

Copyright © 2021 by "Jay" Joseph P. Simala

The author makes this book available as a free download at ChristianGathering.org. You are permitted to reproduce and transmit, but not alter or sell, all or parts of this document.

ISBN: 978-1-7344800-4-7 (paperback)

Unless otherwise noted, all Scripture quotations have been taken from the Christian Standard Bible®, Copyright © 2017 by Holman Bible Publishers. Used by permission. Christian Standard Bible® and CSB® are federally registered trademarks of Holman Bible Publishers.

Design by Renée Yearwood/reneeyearwood.com

Copyediting by Christi McGuire/christimcguire.com

To those who love others
with the love of Christ.

About the Author & ChristianGathering.org

Jay Simala is husband to Lyndsey and father of four children. He is a pastor and an educator in Christian universities. He completed degrees in pastoral ministry (MDiv) and in counseling-psychology (MA) from Trinity Evangelical Divinity School, in business (BBA and MBA) from the University of Wisconsin, and in higher education (PhD) from Loyola University Chicago.

ChristianGathering.org is a website that equips Christians to start, strengthen, and multiply churches. On the website you will find:

- **A free download of this book**—both for your private use and for you to use with others, whether for one-on-one meetings, in Bible studies, or when teaching larger groups.
- Free downloads of **The Discipleship Series**, a curriculum that explains how to follow Jesus in the diverse contexts of our lives: church, family, neighborhood, work, and broader society. The study guides will help to establish you in the core teachings of the Christian faith, so that you can pass along these truths to others (2 Tim. 2:2). The lessons are designed for studying God's Word during a weekly gathering with other Christians, not simply for individual study.
- Free downloads of **The Equipping Series**, a curriculum that trains men and women how to lead within smaller gatherings of believers, like neighborhood house churches.
- Information about **how to start and lead a church in a home under the supervision of your church's leaders**—for family members, friends, and neighbors.
- How to contact Jay.

Contents

Introduction 6

Progress Page 7

Lesson One: Overview of the Book 9

Lesson Two: From God's Initiation to Our Response 21

Lesson Three: God Reveals Himself to Us 27

Lesson Four: We Reject God's Rule in Our Lives 33

Lesson Five: God Responds to Our Disobedience 39

Lesson Six: God Provides the Gift of Jesus 45

Lesson Seven: We Turn to God and Are Baptized 51

Lesson Eight: We Receive the Holy Spirit 57

Lesson Nine: We Are Christians 63

Lesson Ten: We Establish Habits for Christian Growth 69

Lesson Eleven: We Are Growing into the Likeness of Jesus ... 75

Lesson Twelve: We Serve Those in Need 81

Lesson Thirteen: We Help Non-Christians to Know God 87

Lesson Fourteen: We Share the Good News with Others 93

Lesson Fifteen: We Help Christians to Know God Better 99

Lesson Sixteen: We Center Our Lives on God 105

Next Steps 110

References 111

Acknowledgments 112

Introduction

I designed this book to be studied with others who want to learn more about the Christian faith or to review its main teachings. More specifically, I wrote this book for two reasons. **First**, I want to help people know how to enter a personal, reconciled relationship with God through Jesus Christ. **Second**, I want to help people know how to pursue God's purposes for their lives, including developing Christlike character, serving others, and helping others to know God. If one or both of these are already obvious to you, then **use this book to help others to understand these truths**.

Here is one approach to starting a study: (1) pray for guidance from God, (2) invite others (such as your neighbors, friends, and family members) to study this book with you, (3) establish a time and place to meet (e.g., Saturday nights from 5 to 7 p.m. at your house or church building), (4) distribute copies of this book (hard copies or the free PDF on my website) before or at the first meeting, and (5) share a meal together each week before you study the lessons. **Another approach**: teach and discuss these lessons to people in your church, community, or other settings (like a jail or prison) to equip them to lead studies of their own. In time, proactively coach them through steps (1) through (5) above.

For all who are discussing this material with others, you will get the most out of this study if you:

- Read the lesson and complete the discussion questions *before* you meet with others to discuss the lesson.
- Be open and honest about your questions, struggles, and desires regarding the Christian faith.

If you are leading a group meeting:

- Encourage others to take turns reading each part of the lesson out loud.
- After someone reads the Scripture verses and discussion questions, encourage group members to share their answers.

Progress Page

Lesson	Date of Completion
One	
Two	
Three	
Four	
Five	
Six	
Seven	
Eight	
Nine	
Ten	
Eleven	
Twelve	
Thirteen	
Fourteen	
Fifteen	
Sixteen	

Lesson One: Overview of the Book[1]

Imagine you are standing before God, the Creator of all people and things, who reveals himself to us in the Bible.

Then consider these questions:

1. On a scale of 0 to 100%, if you died today, how certain are you that you would spend eternity with God in heaven?
2. If God were to ask you, "Why should I allow you to spend eternity with me?" what would you say?[2]
3. How do you enter a personal relationship with God? Or, put differently, how does someone become a Christian?

Pause to answer these questions in the space below. Also consider asking these questions of others.[3]

1.

2.

3.

---

[1] This lesson is also available online at ChristianGathering.org/the-path-to-god.
[2] I adapted questions one and two above from D. James Kennedy's diagnostic questions found in his book and training program called *Evangelism Explosion*.
[3] When I ask people these questions in university or church settings, I then encourage them to ask these questions of others in their networks. It is quite common that they find that the majority of their friends and family members are unsure of the status of their relationship with God. So, for example, if you have children who are old enough to understand questions like these, ask them the questions, stop talking, and then listen closely.

If you lack assurance that you are in a right relationship with God and will live with him forever, this lesson will clarify how you can begin a relationship with him. *If you have assurance* of your salvation, this lesson will clarify the proper reasons for assurance of salvation and how you can share these truths with others. Either way, God calls us to understand and embrace the following truths:

1. God is the Creator, Lord, and Provider.

> "The God who made the world and everything in it—he is Lord of heaven and earth—does not live in shrines made by hands. Neither is he served by human hands, as though he needed anything, since he himself gives everyone life and breath and all things." (Acts 17:24–25)

As Creator, God made all people and things, and therefore he alone is worthy of our highest love, worship, and commitment (Acts 14:15; 17:24; Rev. 4:11). As Lord, he rules over his creation and commands us to obey his laws, which he reveals to us in the Bible (Ps. 103:19; Acts 17:24; 2 Tim. 3:16–17). And as Provider, he showers us with good things, such as life, food, family, friends, and countless other gifts (Acts 14:17; 17:25; James 1:17). God is perfect in his very being and in all his ways, and we are not (Deut. 32:4; Ps. 11:7; Rev. 4:8).

2. We sin against God. Therefore, we deserve his eternal judgment.

- "For all have sinned and fall short of the glory of God." (Rom. 3:23)
- "For the wages of sin is death." (Rom. 6:23)

All of us have sinned against God, and we are falling short of his glorious perfection (Rom. 3:23). Put simply, sin is disobeying God's commandments in our thoughts, words, and actions (Rom. 3:9–20; 1 John 3:4). Sin is also an act of rebellion against God and his authority (Isa. 1:2; Jer. 3:13). But the heart or essence of sin is that we value other people and things more than God himself, which is idolatry (Rom. 1:25; Col. 3:5).

Whether we commit sins such as vanity, greed, or lying, every sin we commit makes us worthy of God's eternal judgment (Rom. 1:18; Gal. 5:19–21; Col. 3:5–6). A wage is what we earn for work that we perform. In light of our sinful thoughts, words, and actions, the wages we earn from God is death—which includes condemnation both in this life and the next (John 3:18; Rom. 6:23; Eph. 2:1). Put differently, because God is holy and just, he will give us exactly what we deserve in judgment, unless we seek and receive his forgiveness (Rom. 2:5; Heb. 9:27).

3. God sent Jesus into the world to die as an atoning sacrifice for sins, and God raised Jesus from the dead.

- "If anyone does sin, we have an advocate with the Father—Jesus Christ the Righteous One. He himself is the atoning sacrifice [the one who took the penalty] for our sins, and not only for ours, but also for those of the whole world." (1 John 2:1–2)
- "For I passed on to you as most important what I also received: that Christ died for our sins according to the Scriptures, that he was buried, that he was raised on the third day according to the Scriptures." (1 Cor. 15:3–4)

Either we will stand alone before God to give an account for our sins, bearing the penalty ourselves (Matt. 10:33; John 3:36). Or we will stand before God with Jesus as our advocate, the one who represents us before God (1 John 2:1). Jesus died on a cross as an atoning sacrifice for sins, bearing the penalty that we deserve, and satisfying God's justice and wrath (Rom. 3:25–26; 1 John 2:2). After three days, God raised Jesus from the dead to declare him innocent and victorious over death, exalting him to his right hand as Lord, Christ, and Savior (Acts 2:24, 36; 5:31; 1 Cor. 15:3–4).

> In answer to question #2 on page 9, Jesus and his saving work (his perfect life, sin-atoning death, and victorious resurrection) is the only bridge to God the Father, not our good works.

4. We must repent (turn from our sins) and trust in Jesus to enter a personal, reconciled relationship with God.

- "Therefore repent and turn back, so that your sins may be wiped out." (Acts 3:19)
- "For you are saved by grace through faith, and this is not from yourselves; it is God's gift—not from works, so that no one can boast." (Eph. 2:8–9)

God offers forgiveness freely to all, but this free gift must be received in order to be applied to our lives (John 1:12; Rom. 6:23).

First, we repent (turn from our sins) by renouncing the ways we value people and things more than God (Acts 3:19; 1 Thess. 1:9). While we should feel sad because of our sins against God, feeling remorse or a sense of regret is not enough. We must proactively turn from sins such as self-centeredness, pride, sexual immorality (e.g., pornography and sex outside of marriage), drunkenness, vanity, greed, and lying.

Second, we trust in Jesus as opposed to trusting in ourselves (John 3:16; Rom. 3:22, 26; Gal. 2:16). Simply acknowledging (or agreeing) in your head that Jesus died and rose from the dead is not enough, for even demons believe those truths. We must trust in Jesus as a person and what he accomplished at the cross. At the same time, we stop trusting in our own good works for salvation. We are saved by grace (God's unmerited favor) through faith (Eph. 2:8–9).

Turning from our sins and trusting in Jesus (taken together) is the way we enter a relationship with God, the way we receive God's grace (Acts 20:21).

> In answer to question #3 on page 9, repentance and trust in Jesus is how we cross the bridge to God the Father—a bridge created by Jesus alone.

5. We receive the gift of the Holy Spirit.

- "Repent and be baptized, each of you, in the name of Jesus Christ for the forgiveness of your sins, and you will receive the gift of the Holy Spirit." (Acts 2:38)
- "But to all who did receive him [Jesus], he gave them the right to be children of God, to those who believe in his name." (John 1:12)

At the moment we turn from our sins and trust in Jesus, God gives us the gift of the Holy Spirit to guide and empower us (Acts 2:38; Rom. 8:14–17). God also forgives us for our sins, adopts us into his family, and sets us apart for himself and his purposes (John 1:12; 1 Cor. 6:11; Eph. 1:7). These blessings come to us instantaneously, though growing into the likeness of Jesus takes a lifetime (Rom. 8:29; 1 Thess. 4:3; Heb. 12:1–2).

6. With the strength God provides, we seek to obey him in every area of our lives, including getting baptized and actively participating in a local church.

- "Therefore we were buried with him by baptism into death, in order that, just as Christ was raised from the dead by the glory of the Father, so we too may walk in newness of life." (Rom. 6:4)
- "And let us consider how to stir up one another to love and good works, not neglecting to gather together, as some are in the habit of doing, but encouraging each other, and all the more as you see the day [of the Lord's return] approaching." (Heb. 10:24–25)

After we become Christians through repentance and trust in Jesus, we publicly testify to our new faith through baptism, which symbolizes that we have died to sin and have been raised to a new life with Jesus (Acts 2:38, 41; Rom. 6:3–4). God empowers us to grow in our faith, particularly as we participate in a local church. Together we celebrate the Lord's Supper, study the Bible, pray to God, minister to others, and sing to God (Acts 2:42–47; 1 Cor. 11:17–34; Col. 3:16; Titus 2:1–15; Heb. 10:24–25).

For Reflection and Discussion

Use these pages to respond to the following questions, so you can process this information with others.

1. Prior to reading this summary of how to begin a relationship with God, how did you answer the questions at the top of page 9?

2. Now that you have read the summary, would you answer the three questions in the same way or differently? Explain.

3. Do you think Jesus is the only way to God the Father? Why or why not?

4. What does it mean *to repent* (as an act of both the mind and the will)? What does it mean *to trust in Jesus*? Viewed together, have you come to God in this way? If not, what obstacles stand in the way?

Responding to This Lesson

Now that you have read and reflected on this summary of the core teachings of the Christian faith, which one of the following categories describes you?

1. You are already a Christian, for you have repented and trusted in Jesus. If so, hopefully this summary strengthened your faith in Jesus, clarified how you can faithfully share these truths with others, and gave you additional reasons to rejoice in your salvation (Hab. 3:18; Philem. 6; 1 John 5:13).

2. You are not a Christian, and *you are not ready* to repent and trust in Jesus. If so, know that the offer of eternal life with God still stands, but no one is guaranteed life tomorrow (1 Tim. 2:3–4; James 4:13–16; 2 Pet. 3:9).

3. You are not a Christian, but *you are ready* to enter a right relationship with God and live with him forever. If so, today is the day of your salvation (Rom. 10:9; 2 Cor. 6:2)! Consider praying a prayer like this:

   > "Dear God, I confess you as my Creator, Lord, and Provider. I have sinned against you in my thoughts, words, and deeds. I therefore deserve nothing but judgment from you. Jesus and his life, death, and resurrection is my only hope for entering a relationship with you. I accept the gift of eternal life by turning away from my sins and trusting in Jesus. Please forgive me of my sins and give me the gift of your Holy Spirit to lead me forever. Jesus is the Lord of my life from now on. I pray this in Jesus's name. Amen."

Additional Information:
Clarifying Your Own (and Others') Responses
to the Three Diagnostic Questions

At the beginning of this lesson, you were asked these three questions:

1. On a scale of 0 to 100%, if you died today, how certain are you that you would spend eternity with God in heaven?

2. If God were to ask you, "Why should I allow you to spend eternity with me?" what would you say?

3. How do you enter a personal relationship with God? Or, put differently, how does someone become a Christian?

From God's perspective, as revealed in the Bible, *you should be concerned* if you answered the three questions in one or more of the following ways:

- Your answer to question #1 fell between 0 and 99%, particularly if you are merely thinking about your own moral shortcomings and/or your perceived moral goodness before God. The Bible is clear: We have all sinned against God (in our thoughts, words, and actions) and are falling short of his will for our lives (Rom. 1:25; 3:23). We cannot earn salvation based on our good works (Eph. 2:8–9; Titus 3:5). It is therefore troubling when people say they are "70% sure" or "85% sure" they will spend eternity with God based on their behavior. In their words, they "still have room for improvement" in their behavior before they can earn (or merit) eternal salvation—which no sinful person can do.[4]

---

[4] It is also troubling when people say they are "100% sure" but their answers to question #2 reveal that their ultimate confidence before God is in their good works, not in Jesus Christ. For all who trust in their good works to obtain salvation, they should have no such confidence (Rom. 3:20; Gal. 3:10).

- Your answer to question #2 outlined your spiritual résumé (your list of moral qualifications) that you would present to God, such as your church attendance, Bible reading, or care for the poor. This also reveals a works-based view of salvation—a view that ignores (or attempts to add to) Jesus Christ and his saving work. Only Jesus and his death and resurrection serve as the basis by which anyone can be reconciled to God and live with him forever (Rom. 3:21–26; 1 Cor. 15:1–4; 2 Cor. 5:21; 1 John 2:1–2).

> The heart of the matter is whether or not you have turned from your sins and trusted in Jesus Christ alone.

- Your answer to question #3 failed to include both (1) repentance (turning from your sins) and (2) trust in Jesus (as opposed to trusting in yourself to gain access to God). Repentance and trust in Jesus Christ—taken together—is the means by which we enter a relationship with God (Mark 1:15; Acts 20:21; Gal. 2:16). It is the way we accept the gift of eternal life, the way we become Christians. Then, by God's grace, we receive the gift of the Holy Spirit, who helps us to grow into the likeness of Jesus (Acts 2:38; Rom. 8:29; Gal. 5:16–26).

Lesson Two: From God's Initiation to Our Response

Overview

In Acts 17:22–34, the apostle Paul teaches us much about God—the God who reveals himself to us in the Bible. In this lesson and throughout the book, we explore the questions, "Who is God?" and "How does God call us to relate to him?"

1. God initiates a relationship with us through his Word.

> Paul stood in the middle of the Areopagus and said: "People of Athens! I see that you are extremely religious in every respect. For as I was passing through and observing the objects of your worship, I even found an altar on which was inscribed: 'To an Unknown God.' Therefore, what you worship in ignorance, this I proclaim to you." (Acts 17:22–23)

God spoke to the people of Athens through the words of the apostle Paul. Today, God continues to speak to us through his written Word, the Bible. However, there are many obstacles to knowing God, such as (1) a lack of knowledge (where we don't know his Word), (2) unconfessed sin (where we value sinning more than God himself), (3) unaddressed pain (where our hurts inappropriately influence our thinking about God), (4) laziness (where we lack the motivation to seek God and his truth), (5) busyness (where we don't create enough time to know God), and (6) isolation from Christian community (where we distance ourselves from growing with others who are seeking to know God). These obstacles are usually interrelated and reinforce one another. But despite our resistance to God, he speaks to us clearly and consistently.

- What obstacles interfere with you seeking God more diligently?
- With help from God and others, what choices can you make to overcome those obstacles?

2. God is the Creator, Lord, and Provider.
- "The God who made the world and everything in it—he is Lord of heaven and earth—does not live in shrines made by hands. Neither is he served by human hands, as though he needed anything, since he himself gives everyone life and breath and all things." (Acts 17:24–25)
- "From one man he has made every nationality to live over the whole earth and has determined their appointed times and the boundaries of where they live. He did this so that they might seek God, and perhaps they might reach out and find him, though he is not far from each one of us." (Acts 17:26–27)
- "For in him we live and move and have our being, as even some of your own poets have said, 'For we are also his offspring.' Since we are God's offspring then, we shouldn't think that the divine nature is like gold or silver or stone, an image fashioned by human art and imagination." (Acts 17:28–29)

It is often tempting to view reality in self-centered ways. But in these verses Paul directs us to the God who created all people and things and, as we will see throughout this book, to the God who is worthy of our deepest love and worship.

> As you read Acts 17:24–29 phrase by phrase, what do you learn (about God, humanity, and how God and humanity relate to one another)?

3. God calls us to repent (turn from our sins) and to trust in him.

- "Therefore, having overlooked the times of ignorance, God now commands all people everywhere to repent, because he has set a day when he is going to judge the world in righteousness by the man he has appointed. He has provided proof of this to everyone by raising him from the dead." (Acts 17:30–31)
- "When they heard about the resurrection of the dead, some began to ridicule him, but others said, 'We'd like to hear from you again about this.' So Paul left their presence. However, some people joined him and believed, including Dionysius the Areopagite, a woman named Damaris, and others with them." (Acts 17:32–34)

Because God is the Creator, Lord, and Provider, he has expectations for our lives, and we are accountable to him (Acts 17:30–31; Heb. 4:13). His most basic commandments are that we repent (turn from our sins) and trust in him and his Son, Jesus Christ, for salvation (Acts 2:38; 20:21; Gal. 2:16). This is how we enter a personal, reconciled relationship with God.

> - From Acts 17:30–34, what do you learn about God? About what he requires of you?
> - What does it mean to "repent" in your own words? What does it mean to "trust in Jesus"?

For Reflection and Discussion

Use the space below to respond to the following questions, to record your prayers to God, and/or to prepare to process this information with others.

1. In one sentence, summarize one of the most important things that you learned in this lesson about God (including his characteristics, words, and/or actions) and how you plan to respond to that truth (in your heart, words, and/or actions). "Because God _____, I will _____."
2. Why are you thankful to God for his work in and around you?
3. Name one or more of your desires that you want to bring to God in prayer (for yourself and/or for others).

Lesson Three: God Reveals Himself to Us

Overview

Three of the most important and repeated truths we discover in the Bible are that God created us, he communicates with us, and he reveals his righteous commandments to us. In this lesson, we explore these truths and their implications for our lives.

1. God created all people and things.

- "In the beginning God created the heavens and the earth." (Gen. 1:1)
- "Then God said, 'Let us make man in our image, according to our likeness. They will rule the fish of the sea, the birds of the sky, the livestock, the whole earth, and the creatures that crawl on the earth.' So God created man in his own image; he created him in the image of God; he created them male and female." (Gen. 1:26–27)
- "God saw all that he had made, and it was very good indeed." (Gen. 1:31)

The first verse of the first book of the Bible teaches us that God is the Creator (Gen. 1:1), and therefore we are mere creatures. Reading on, we learn that God created us in his image (in his likeness) to rule on his behalf (vv. 26–27). At this point in the story, there was no sin in the world, for everything that God made "was very good indeed" (v. 31; see Gen. 2:25).

- How do you respond to the claim that you have a Creator? With agreement, interest, resistance, or something else?
- Given that God made you in his image, what would it look like for you to represent him well in different areas of your life?

2. God communicates with us.

- "For his invisible attributes, that is, his eternal power and divine nature, have been clearly seen since the creation of the world, being understood through what he has made. As a result, people are without excuse." (Rom. 1:20)
- "All Scripture is inspired by God and is profitable for teaching, for rebuking, for correcting, for training in righteousness." (2 Tim. 3:16)
- "In these last days, he [God the Father] has spoken to us by his Son. God has appointed him heir of all things and made the universe through him." (Heb.1:2)

From the beginning of the Bible to the end, we learn that God is a talking God. God speaks to us through the natural world (Rom. 1:20). He speaks to us through his written Word, the Bible, and through those who faithfully explain it (2 Tim. 3:16). And he speaks to us through the person of Jesus Christ (Heb. 1:2). For each of us, the great opportunity and challenge is to listen.

> - What interferes with your ability or willingness to listen to God more attentively?
> - What might God be saying to you at this time in your life?

3. God reveals his righteous commandments to us.

- "The Rock—his work is perfect; all his ways are just. A faithful God, without bias, he is righteous and true." (Deut. 32:4)
- "For the LORD is our Judge, the LORD is our Lawgiver, the LORD is our King. He will save us." (Isa. 33:22)
- "My little children, I am writing you these things so that you may not sin. But if anyone does sin, we have an advocate with the Father—Jesus Christ the righteous one. He himself is the atoning sacrifice for our sins, and not only for ours, but also for those of the whole world." (1 John 2:1–2)

God is righteous in that he is the ultimate standard for what is right and good, and he is perfectly pure in all of his thoughts, words, and actions (Deut. 32:4; 1 John 1:5). Flowing from his perfect righteousness, he establishes, reveals, and enforces his righteous commands as humanity's Judge, Lawgiver, and King (Isa. 33:22; 1 Tim. 1:17). Each of us falls short of his righteous standards (Rom. 3:10, 23), which is why we need to trust in and receive forgiveness through Jesus Christ—the Holy and Righteous One who died for sins (1 John 2:1–2; Acts 3:14–15).

- To what extent and in what ways are you tempted to reject God's authority and commands? Why?
- What does it mean that Jesus is the "atoning sacrifice" for sins?

For Reflection and Discussion

Use the space below to respond to the following questions, to record your prayers to God, and/or to prepare to process this information with others.

1. In one sentence, summarize one of the most important things that you learned in this lesson about God (including his characteristics, words, and/or actions) and how you plan to respond to that truth (in your heart, words, and/or actions). "Because God _____, I will _____."
2. Why are you thankful to God for his work in and around you?
3. Name one or more of your desires that you want to bring to God in prayer (for yourself and/or for others).

Lesson Four:
We Reject God's Rule in Our Lives

Overview

We need to be careful how we define our biggest problems in life, for that will dictate the solutions we pursue. For example, we may be tempted to believe that our biggest problem in life is any one of the following: dating or marital problems, distant or rebellious children, or a lack of a satisfying job. And while these are legitimate challenges we face, our biggest problems in life are our personal sin against God and the consequences of that sin.

1. We rebel against God and his authority.

- "Sing a song of wisdom, for God is King of the whole earth. God reigns over the nations; God is seated on his holy throne." (Ps. 47:7–8)
- "And the LORD God commanded the man, 'You are free to eat from any tree of the garden, but you must not eat from the tree of the knowledge of good and evil, for on the day you eat from it, you will certainly die.'" (Gen. 2:16–17)
- "The woman saw that the tree was good for food and delightful to look at, and that it was desirable for obtaining wisdom. So she took some of its fruit and ate it; she also gave some to her husband, who was with her, and he ate it." (Gen. 3:6)

God is the Creator, and he is the King over all people and things (Ps. 47:7–8). He therefore has the right to command us to obey (Gen. 2:16–17). However, just like the first human beings, Adam and Eve, we rebel against God and reject his authority (Gen. 3:6). Put simply, we think we know better, and we prefer the temporary pleasures of sin more than lasting joy in God and his ways.

- Identify a time when you rebelled against a legitimate authority, other than God, such as one or both of your parents. At the time, in what ways were you tempted to believe that your way was better?
- Identify a time when you rebelled against God's will. At the time, in what ways were you tempted to think that you knew better than God?

2. We are sinful, and we sin.

- "Indeed, I was guilty when I was born; I was sinful when my mother conceived me." (Ps. 51:5)
- "Therefore, put to death what belongs to your earthly nature: sexual immorality, impurity, lust, evil desire, and greed, which is idolatry." (Col. 3:5)
- "So it is sin to know the good and yet not do it." (James 4:17)

Our tendencies to rebel against God run deep within us. Each of us is born into a sinful condition that extends to every part of who we are: our desires, values, thoughts, emotions, and behaviors (Ps. 51:5). This inner disposition leads us to commit specific sins against God.

We think and do things that we should not, which are *sins of commission* (Col. 3:5). They include hatred, greed, pride, gossip, and vanity. We also refuse to think and do what we should, which are *sins of omission* (James 4:17). They include a lack of faith, a lack of hope, a lack of self-control, and a lack of care for those in need.

- Which sins of commission do you struggle with? For each one you list, what makes it so attractive to you?
- Which sins of omission do you struggle with? For each one you list, what makes it so attractive to you?

3. We overvalue people and things.

- "For the LORD is great and is highly praised; he is feared above all gods. For all the gods of the peoples are idols, but the LORD made the heavens." (Ps. 96:4–5)
- "They exchanged the truth of God for a lie, and worshiped and served what has been created instead of the Creator, who is praised forever. Amen." (Rom. 1:25)

No person or thing is more valuable and worthy of our worship than God himself (Ps. 96:4–5). Tragically, however, we value people and things more than God (Rom. 1:25). This is idolatry, which is the act of valuing, loving, desiring, enjoying, trusting in, or hoping in someone or something *more than God*.

Relational idols are the people we value more than God, such as family members, friends, and celebrities. *Non-relational idols* are the things we value more than God, such as money, entertainment, and possessions. Whether we are consciously aware of it or not, we enter into relationships with these idols to lead us into the future, though they have no power to give us eternal life and joy.

Given our struggle with sin, our only hope is Jesus Christ—the one who never sinned, the one who paid the penalty for sins at the cross (2 Cor. 5:21).

- To which relational idols do you turn? What false promises does each one offer you?
- To which non-relational idols do you turn? What false promises does each one offer you?
- Why does humanity need Jesus? How should we respond to him?

For Reflection and Discussion

Use the space below to respond to the following questions, to record your prayers to God, and/or to prepare to process this information with others.

1. In one sentence, summarize one of the most important things that you learned in this lesson about God (including his characteristics, words, and/or actions) and how you plan to respond to that truth (in your heart, words, and/or actions). "Because God _____, I will _____."
2. Why are you thankful to God for his work in and around you?
3. Name one or more of your desires that you want to bring to God in prayer (for yourself and/or for others).

Lesson Five: God Responds to Our Disobedience

Overview

While it may be uncomfortable to consider, listening to how God responds to our self-centered, sinful ways is a necessary step toward being reconciled to him. Put differently, we need to hear *the bad news* of God's responses to our sins before *the good news* of Jesus's death and resurrection makes any sense. Despite our sins, God expresses his love for us in a variety of ways—most profoundly in sending Jesus to the cross to die on our behalf (John 3:16; Rom. 5:8).

1. God explains the immediate effects of sin.

    - "Then the man and his wife heard the sound of the LORD God walking in the garden at the time of the evening breeze, and they hid from the LORD God among the trees of the garden." (Gen. 3:8)
    - "If we say, 'We have no sin,' we are deceiving ourselves, and the truth is not in us." (1 John 1:8)
    - "Therefore God delivered them over in the desires of their hearts to sexual impurity, so that their bodies were degraded among themselves." (Rom. 1:24)

The effects of sin are diverse. First, we run from God, oppose him, or deny his existence. For example, after Adam and Eve sinned, they attempted to hide themselves from God (as if that were possible!), because they were filled for the first time with moral shame (Gen. 3:8). Second, we often deny our sins as an act of self-deception (1 John 1:8). Third, we engage in more sin, as God hands us over to our sinful desires (Rom. 1:24, 26, 28).

- In what ways do you flee from, oppose, or deny God?
- In what ways do you lie to yourself about your sins and their effects on your life? For example, how do you deny, minimize, or justify your sins?

2. God declares the ultimate effect of sin: death.

- "You will eat bread by the sweat of your brow until you return to the ground, since you were taken from it. For you are dust, and you will return to dust." (Gen. 3:19)
- "And you were dead in your trespasses and sins in which you previously walked." (Eph. 2:1–2)
- "Because of your hardened and unrepentant heart you are storing up wrath for yourself in the day of wrath, when God's righteous judgment is revealed." (Rom. 2:5)

As part of God's spoken word of judgment to Adam and Eve (Gen. 3:16–19), he declared that Adam would die physically: "You will return to dust" (v. 19). In time, Adam did die physically (Gen. 5:5), just as we all do in this life (Heb. 9:27). Figuratively speaking, the apostle Paul used the word *dead* to describe our relationship to God apart from Jesus Christ (Eph. 2:1). Not only are we unresponsive to God and lifeless, but we also stand condemned and are alienated from him, all because of our sins. But the ultimate judgment of God is eternal punishment from him—an ongoing, unending, conscious death (Rom. 2:5)—for all who will not turn from their sins and trust in Jesus.

- How often and in what ways do you think about your physical death? Why do many people avoid doing so?
- What does it mean to be "dead in one's sins"? Does this describe you? Why or why not?

3. God expresses his love.

- "But I tell you, love your enemies and pray for those who persecute you, so that you may be children of your Father in heaven. For he causes his sun to rise on the evil and the good, and sends rain on the righteous and the unrighteous." (Matt. 5:44–45)
- "But God proves his own love for us in that while we were still sinners, Christ died for us." (Rom. 5:8)
- "Deal with your servant based on your faithful love; teach me your statutes." (Ps. 119:124)

Despite the terrible consequences of our sins, God's love is greater. He expresses his love through giving us everyday blessings, such as life and breath, food and water, family and friends, and a general sense of morality (Matt. 5:44–45). God expressed his love for humanity most profoundly by sending his Son into the world to die (Rom. 5:8). Jesus, who committed no sin, died on a cross to satisfy God's wrath against sinners (Rom. 3:21–26). And God expresses his love by teaching us his Word (Ps. 119:124). In his grace, he then keeps his people in his love as he helps us to obey (Rom. 8:28–39; Jude 1).

- What everyday blessings from God make you grateful?
- God sent Jesus into the world to die. How is that God's supreme act of love for humanity?

For Reflection and Discussion

Use the space below to respond to the following questions, to record your prayers to God, and/or to prepare to process this information with others.

1. In one sentence, summarize one of the most important things that you learned in this lesson about God (including his characteristics, words, and/or actions) and how you plan to respond to that truth (in your heart, words, and/or actions). "Because God _____, I will _____."
2. Why are you thankful to God for his work in and around you?
3. Name one or more of your desires that you want to bring to God in prayer (for yourself and/or for others).

Lesson Six: God Provides the Gift of Jesus

Overview

In the previous lessons, we discovered that our biggest problems in life are our personal sin against God and the consequences of that sin. Without God's loving, merciful, and gracious intervention, there would be no hope for us. For our eternal good, God sent his Son into the world as his supreme act of love. Jesus lived a perfect life, satisfied God's justice at the cross, and rose from the dead victorious—paving the only way to God.

1. Jesus lived a righteous life.

- "The angel replied to her: 'The Holy Spirit will come upon you, and the power of the Most High will overshadow you. Therefore, the holy one to be born will be called the Son of God.'" (Luke 1:35)
- "When Peter saw this, he addressed the people: 'Fellow Israelites...You denied the Holy and Righteous One and asked to have a murderer released to you. You killed the source of life, whom God raised from the dead; we are witnesses of this.'" (Acts 3:12, 14–15)
- "For Christ also suffered for sins once for all, the righteous for the unrighteous, that he might bring you to God. He was put to death in the flesh but made alive by the Spirit." (1 Pet. 3:18)

Jesus was born in a sinless condition, unlike every other human being. He did not inherit guilt or corruption from Adam, because Jesus was conceived by a miracle of the Holy Spirit (Luke 1:35). Therefore, he had no desire or inclination to sin. Jesus is perfectly righteous, in that he kept (and keeps) all his Father's commandments (Acts 3:14). This righteousness qualified him to atone for our sins, for Jesus is the Righteous One who suffered for unrighteous people to bring them to God (1 Pet. 3:18).

- In what ways are you unrighteous? Apart from Jesus, what are the consequences of your unrighteousness?
- Why was Jesus's perfect righteousness necessary for him to serve as a sacrifice for humanity's sins?

2. Jesus died in our place.

- "God presented him as an atoning sacrifice by his blood, through faith, to demonstrate his righteousness, because in his restraint God passed over the sins previously committed." (Rom. 3:25)
- "For even the Son of Man did not come to be served, but to serve, and to give his life as a ransom for many." (Mark 10:45)
- "For if, while we were enemies, we were reconciled to God through the death of his Son, then how much more, having been reconciled, will we be saved by his life." (Rom. 5:10)

In his great love, God sent Jesus to the cross to die as an "atoning sacrifice," an act that meets the demands of God's justice and results in forgiveness for God's people (Rom. 3:25). From a different perspective, Jesus gave his life as a ransom, which releases people from the bondage of sin and death (Mark 10:45). Based on Jesus's death and through our faith, we are reconciled to God, which marks the end of our broken relationship with God. This saves us *from* God's wrath and saves us *to* a reconciled relationship with God (Rom. 5:9–11).

- In your own words, what are some of the reasons why God the Father sent Jesus into the world to die?
- What would you say to someone who claims that Jesus's death and resurrection were unnecessary for us to gain eternal life with God?

3. Jesus rose from the dead victorious.
- "Though he was delivered up according to God's determined plan and foreknowledge, you used lawless people to nail him to a cross and kill him. God raised him up, ending the pains of death, because it was not possible for him to be held by death." (Acts 2:23–24)
- "But as it is, Christ has been raised from the dead, the firstfruits of those who have fallen asleep." (1 Cor. 15:20)
- "[God the Father] made us alive with Christ even though we were dead in trespasses. You are saved by grace! He also raised us up with him and seated us with him in the heavens in Christ Jesus." (Eph. 2:5–6)

God raised Jesus from the dead to declare him innocent and to vindicate him. Death had no final claim on Jesus, for he was sinless (Acts 2:23–24). The resurrected Jesus is described as "the firstfruits" (1 Cor. 15:20), the first gathering of a crop that points to what the rest of the crop will look like. God, in and through the resurrection of Jesus, raises people to life—alive to God and raised up with Christ (Eph. 2:5–6). And God raised Jesus to secure our resurrection bodies. So just as Jesus has a perfect, glorified body, he will also give Christians perfect, glorified bodies in the life to come (Phil. 3:21).

- Why did God the Father raise Jesus from the dead?
- Which better describes you—alive to God or dead to God? What evidence do you see of one or the other?

For Reflection and Discussion

Use the space below to respond to the following questions, to record your prayers to God, and/or to prepare to process this information with others.

1. In one sentence, summarize one of the most important things that you learned in this lesson about God (including his characteristics, words, and/or actions) and how you plan to respond to that truth (in your heart, words, and/or actions). "Because God _____, I will _____."
2. Why are you thankful to God for his work in and around you?
3. Name one or more of your desires that you want to bring to God in prayer (for yourself and/or for others).

Lesson Seven: We Turn to God and Are Baptized

Overview

In order to be reconciled to God, we must (1) repent (turn from our sins) and (2) trust in Jesus alone (not our good works). Taken together, theologians call repentance and trust the doctrine of *conversion* (Acts 20:21). When we repent and trust in Jesus, we gain eternal life with God. We then testify to our new faith through baptism, which symbolizes our death to self and our new life in union with and submission to the God of the Bible.

1. We repent (turn from our sins).

- "The time is fulfilled, and the kingdom of God has come near. Repent and believe the good news!" (Mark 1:15)
- "And many who had become believers came confessing and disclosing their practices, while many of those who had practiced magic collected their books and burned them in front of everyone." (Acts 19:18–19)

Jesus called people to repent (turn from sin) and trust in him (Mark 1:15). Repentance often begins with grieving over our sinful thoughts, words, and behaviors, but we may not be ready to turn away from them. Perhaps we are sad and embarrassed that others know about our sins. Repentance, however, "is an intellectual *understanding* (that sin is wrong), an emotional *approval* of the teachings of Scripture regarding sin (a sorrow for sin and a hatred of it), and a *personal decision* to turn from it (a renouncing of sin and a decision of the will to forsake it and lead a life of obedience to Christ instead)."[5] In Acts 19, for example, the new believers in the Lord Jesus burned their books of magic spells, turning away from that sin. In a like manner, God calls each of us to turn proactively from the ways that we disobey him.

- How would you explain repentance in your own words?
- Though no one is perfect, have you turned from your sins? If so, how and when did that happen? If not, why not?

---

[5] Grudem, *Systematic Theology*, 865–866 (italics his).

2. We trust in Jesus.

- "I testified to both Jews and Greeks about repentance toward God and faith in our Lord Jesus." (Acts 20:21)
- "You believe that God is one. Good! Even the demons believe—and they shudder." (James 2:19)
- "For God loved the world in this way: He gave his one and only Son, so that everyone who believes in him will not perish but have eternal life." (John 3:16)

Repentance is the decision to turn *from sin* and turn *to God*, by faith in Jesus (Acts 20:21; see Gal. 2:16). We turn *from* something, and we turn *to* God and Jesus Christ, in faith. In that way, repentance and trust are inseparable—two sides of the same moral coin. To trust in Jesus, knowledge is required, but it is not enough. It is possible to know things about God but not to be in a reconciled relationship with him (James 2:19). Satan himself certainly "believes" that Jesus died and rose from the dead, and yet Satan hates God and hates God's people. Saving faith, however, is trust in Jesus as our only hope to live with God. It is a relational trust that clings to Jesus and his saving work on the cross while simultaneously renouncing our self-righteousness. This is the faith that results in eternal life (John 3:16).

- What is saving faith? Do you have it? Why or why not?
- How does faith then lead to concrete action in your life? For example, "Because I trust God, I will _____."

3. We testify to our faith through baptism.

- "Go, therefore, and make disciples of all nations, baptizing them in the name of the Father and of the Son and of the Holy Spirit." (Matt. 28:19)
- "Therefore we were buried with him by baptism into death, in order that, just as Christ was raised from the dead by the glory of the Father, so we too may walk in newness of life." (Rom. 6:4)

Jesus instructed his disciples to baptize new followers in the one "name" (which is singular, not plural) of the triune God: Father, Son, and Holy Spirit (Matt. 28:19). "Baptism pictures a person being buried with Christ (submersion under water) and being raised to new life with Christ (emergence from water)"[6] (Rom. 6:4). In the Bible, people were baptized *after* they repented and believed, *not before* (Acts 2:38, 41). If you were "baptized" before you turned from your sins and trusted in Jesus alone, then you merely got wet.

- What is Christian baptism? What does it represent?
- Were you baptized *after* you repented and trusted in Jesus alone? If so, share your story of becoming a Christian and your subsequent baptism. If not, do you believe you need to be baptized (for the first time)? Explain.

---

[6] *ESV Study Bible*, 2,167.

For Reflection and Discussion

Use the space below to respond to the following questions, to record your prayers to God, and/or to prepare to process this information with others.

1. In one sentence, summarize one of the most important things that you learned in this lesson about God (including his characteristics, words, and/or actions) and how you plan to respond to that truth (in your heart, words, and/or actions). "Because God _____, I will _____."
2. Why are you thankful to God for his work in and around you?
3. Name one or more of your desires that you want to bring to God in prayer (for yourself and/or for others).

Lesson Eight: We Receive the Holy Spirit

Overview

Jesus referred to the Holy Spirit as the Counselor (sometimes translated as the Helper or Advocate), whom the Father would send to his people (John 14:16). The Holy Spirit was with Jesus's original disciples, and God gives the gift of the Holy Spirit to all of us who turn from our sins and trust in Jesus (Acts 1:8; 2:38; Gal. 3:14). The Holy Spirit sets us apart, guides us, and empowers us.

1. The Holy Spirit sets us apart and transforms us.

- "Peter, an apostle of Jesus Christ: To those chosen… according to the foreknowledge of God the Father, *through the sanctifying work of the Spirit*, to be obedient and to be sprinkled with the blood of Jesus Christ. May grace and peace be multiplied to you." (1 Pet. 1:1–2)
- "But the fruit of the Spirit is love, joy, peace, patience, kindness, goodness, faithfulness, gentleness, and self-control. The law is not against such things." (Gal. 5:22–23)

The Holy Spirit sets us apart from the old life we lived apart from God to a new life that we live with God. The apostle Peter describes this as "the sanctifying work [or setting apart] of the Spirit" (1 Pet. 1:2). From one perspective, this work is already complete, since all Christians are set apart for God and his purposes. From another, there is much work for the Holy Spirit to do in and through us. For example, the Spirit of God produces the transformation of our character, which is one of the ways we participate in his work (Gal. 5:22–23).

- How have Christians already been sanctified or set apart? Set apart from what? By whom? To what?
- What aspects of your own character do you want to change? How would doing so affect your life with God and others?

2. The Holy Spirit guides us.

- "For all those led by God's Spirit are God's sons. For you did not receive a spirit of slavery to fall back into fear. Instead, you received the Spirit of adoption, by whom we cry out, '*Abba*, Father!' The Spirit himself testifies together with our spirit that we are God's children." (Rom. 8:14–16)
- "With all humility and gentleness, with patience, bearing with one another in love, making every effort to keep the unity of the Spirit through the bond of peace." (Eph. 4:2–3)

The Holy Spirit teaches, brings to remembrance Jesus's words, and declares things to come (John 14:26; 15:26). He assures Christians that they are sons and daughters of God, and he is the one by whom Christians cry out to God as "*Abba*, Father!" (*Abba* means "father" in Aramaic) (Rom. 8:14–16). God calls Christians to a relational unity that is produced by the Spirit (Eph. 4:2–3). The Spirit's ministry also unites believers to serve others, share possessions, give money to advance God's work, proclaim the good news that Jesus died and rose from the dead, and, ultimately, to worship God (Acts 2:42–47; 4:32–37).

> - In what areas of your life is the Holy Spirit leading you into the truth? What does that look like in practice?
> - Are you assured that you are God's child and have eternal life? Why or why not?

3. The Holy Spirit empowers us.

- "A manifestation of the Spirit is given to each person for the common good. One and the same Spirit is active in all these, distributing to each person as he wills." (1 Cor. 12:7, 11)
- "But you will receive power when the Holy Spirit has come on you, and you will be my witnesses in Jerusalem, in all Judea and Samaria, and to the end of the earth." (Acts 1:8)

Even after we become Christians, we will struggle with sin until the day we die. However, the Holy Spirit empowers us to overcome sin. God promises that those who fight against sin by God's Spirit will live forever (Rom. 8:13). The Holy Spirit also empowers us for service. Each person of the Trinity participates in empowering Christians for service in the church (Rom. 12:3–8; 1 Cor. 12:4–11; 1 Pet. 4:10–11), but the Holy Spirit's role is particularly on display in 1 Corinthians 12. We learn that the Spirit apportions various gifts for the common good (v. 7) and to each as he wills (v. 11). At the center of the Spirit's work, he empowers us to speak God's Word boldly (Acts 4:31), particularly as we witness to and for Jesus (Acts 1:8).

- With God's help, how can you fight against sin in your life? What does it look like to pursue personal holiness?
- How do you want to serve more actively in a local church?

For Reflection and Discussion

Use the space below to respond to the following questions, to record your prayers to God, and/or to prepare to process this information with others.

1. In one sentence, summarize one of the most important things that you learned in this lesson about God (including his characteristics, words, and/or actions) and how you plan to respond to that truth (in your heart, words, and/or actions). "Because God _____, I will _____."
2. Why are you thankful to God for his work in and around you?
3. Name one or more of your desires that you want to bring to God in prayer (for yourself and/or for others).

Lesson Nine: We Are Christians

Overview

Once someone becomes a Christian by turning from his or her sins and trusting in Jesus, it is a time for celebration! For all of us who are Christians—in Christ by the power of the Holy Spirit—God brought us to life, declared us righteous, and adopted us into his family. That is how God sees us. Therefore, that is how we should see ourselves.

1. God brought us to life.

- "But to all who did receive him, he gave them the right to be children of God, to those who believe in his name, who were born, not of natural descent, or of the will of the flesh, or of the will of man, but of God." (John 1:12–13)
- "And when you were dead in trespasses and in the uncircumcision of your flesh, he made you alive with him and forgave us all our trespasses." (Col. 2:13)

Those who are spiritually dead (unresponsive to God and under the power and penalty of sin) do not come to life on their own. So God must initiate toward people and bring them to life. Just as Jesus raised Lazarus from the dead in the physical realm (John 11:38–44), God brings his people to life in the spiritual realm (John 1:13). God brought us to life with Jesus, the one who died for our sins and whom God raised from the dead (Col. 2:12–14; Eph. 2:4–7). While the transformation of our character is not immediate, we practice righteous living (1 John 2:29), and we love our Christian brothers and sisters (1 John 4:7). This is some of the evidence of God's supernatural work in our lives—evidence of new, eternal life.

- When you became a Christian, in what ways did it feel like you came alive to God? For example, how did you begin to think differently? How did your desires change?
- What are some of the implications for our lives now that we are alive to God? In other words, how does a person die to sin (and the old way of life) and live for God?

2. God declared us righteous.

- "God presented him to demonstrate his righteousness at the present time, so that he would be righteous and declare righteous the one who has faith in Jesus." (Rom. 3:26)
- "He [God the Father] made the one who did not know sin [Jesus] to be sin for us, so that in him [Jesus] we might become the righteousness of God." (2 Cor. 5:21)

At the moment we become Christians, *God the Father declares us righteous* in his sight, even though *we are unrighteous* in our thoughts, words, and actions. Put simply, he pronounces unrighteous people to be righteous, and that declaration is called *justification*. Because we cannot meet God's standard on our own, the perfect righteousness must come from someone else. Jesus is the Righteous One who never sinned (Acts 3:14; 1 Pet. 3:18).

And so begins the great exchange for all who trust in Jesus (Rom. 3:25–26; 2 Cor. 5:21). Based on how Jesus's death satisfied God's justice and wrath, God credits our unrighteousness to Jesus (even though he is perfectly righteous). And based on Jesus's perfect obedience to God, God credits Jesus's righteousness to us (even though we are not righteous). Jesus alone earned and secured our right standing before God. Then, with strength and guidance from God, we begin to grow into the likeness of Jesus.

- How would you explain justification in your own words?
- Can someone earn justification? Why or why not?

3. God adopted us into his family.

- "He [God the Father] predestined us to be adopted as sons through Jesus Christ for himself, according to the good pleasure of his will." (Eph. 1:5)
- "When the time came to completion, God sent his Son, born of a woman, born under the law, to redeem those under the law, so that we might receive adoption as sons. And because you are sons, God sent the Spirit of his Son into our hearts, crying, '*Abba*, Father!'" (Gal. 4:4–6)

Prior to becoming Christians, we were outside of God's family, but God the Father adopted us. He "predestined us to be adopted," which was the result of his great love (Eph. 1:4–5). God redeemed us (paying our moral debts and setting us free from our slavery to sin) by sending Jesus to the cross (Gal. 4:4–5). All of this was necessary for us to receive adoption into God's family. When God adopts us into his family, we cry out to him by the Holy Spirit he provides (Gal. 4:6). We immediately join a family with our brothers and sisters in Christ—a worldwide, eternal family.

- Describe your life prior to God adopting you into his family. What was it like to be Father-less in your life?
- What are some of the joys of relating to God as your Father? What are some of the joys of being a part of a family with brothers and sisters in Christ?

For Reflection and Discussion

Use the space below to respond to the following questions, to record your prayers to God, and/or to prepare to process this information with others.

1. In one sentence, summarize one of the most important things that you learned in this lesson about God (including his characteristics, words, and/or actions) and how you plan to respond to that truth (in your heart, words, and/or actions). "Because God _____, I will _____."
2. Why are you thankful to God for his work in and around you?
3. Name one or more of your desires that you want to bring to God in prayer (for yourself and/or for others).

Lesson Ten: We Establish Habits for Christian Growth

Overview

For all who are Christians, God the Father is the one who starts, continues, and completes his work in us (Phil. 1:6; 2:13). For our part, we actively participate in a local church, which is essential for our growth. Together with our brothers and sisters in Christ, we take the Lord's Supper (ideally as part of extended fellowship meals), study the Bible, pray, give and receive encouragement, and serve one another (Acts 2:42–47; 1 Cor. 11:17–34; Heb. 10:24–25; 1 Pet. 4:10–11). These are some of the primary ways that we grow in our faith and partner with God as he works in and through our lives.

1. We participate in a church.

The church of Jesus Christ does not consist of buildings or land or programs. Instead, the church consists of people—God's people. Christians gather as churches (or "assemblies" in God's presence) in public gatherings and in private gatherings (like homes) to glorify God and pursue his purposes (Acts 2:46; 5:42; 20:20; Rom. 16:5; 1 Cor. 1:2). Below is a list of ways that we experience and express our faith in the context of a local church. More specifically, they are the corporate habits that honor God, contribute to personal growth, and benefit others.

1. We teach and are taught God's Word in a local church (Acts 2:42).
2. We pray together in a local church (Acts 2:42).
3. We celebrate the Lord's Supper in a local church, ideally as part of a fellowship meal with Christians (Luke 22:14–20; Acts 2:42, 46; 20:7; 1 Cor. 11:17–34).
4. We worship God in a local church (Acts 2:43, 47; Eph. 5:19–20).
5. We give and receive resources in a local church (Acts 2:44–45; 4:32–37).
6. We follow our leaders in a local church (Heb. 13:7, 17).
7. We hear, proclaim, and explain the gospel in a local church (Acts 4:33; Rom. 1:15–17).
8. We use our spiritual gifts to serve one another in a local church (Rom. 12:1–8; 1 Cor. 12:1–11, 28; 1 Pet. 4:10–11).

- How would you respond to someone who said, "I believe I am a Christian, but I do not need to participate in a local church"?
- What, if anything, is preventing you from becoming more committed to and more active within a local church?

2. We establish habits of Bible study.

- "They devoted themselves to the apostles' teaching, to the fellowship, to the breaking of bread, and to prayer." (Acts 2:42)
- "For whatever was written in the past was written for our instruction, so that we may have hope through endurance and through the encouragement from the Scriptures." (Rom. 15:4)

We hear from God through his Word in a variety of ways. Publicly, we listen to God's Word read aloud, preached, explained, and applied (Rev. 1:3; 2 Tim. 4:2; Acts 2:42). Privately, we study, meditate on, memorize, and apply the Bible (Josh. 1:8; Pss. 1:1–2; 119:11). And we use God's Word to shape our prayers to God (see, for example, Matt. 6:9–13). As we do so, God speaks to us, and we receive the instruction and encouragement we need to keep going in our faith (Rom. 15:4). In these ways and more, Christians are Word-centered.[7]

- What obstacles interfere with you listening to God through his Word? What choices can you make to overcome those obstacles?
- What is your plan for "taking in" God's Word more regularly (including private Bible reading)?

---

[7] Read *Spiritual Disciplines for the Christian Life*, by Donald S. Whitney, specifically chapters 2 and 3.

3. We express our desires to God in prayer.

> "Therefore, you should pray like this: 'Our Father in heaven, your name be honored as holy. Your kingdom come. Your will be done on earth as it is in heaven. Give us today our daily bread. And forgive us our debts, as we also have forgiven our debtors. And do not bring us into temptation [or testing], but deliver us from the evil one.'" (Matt. 6:9–13)

Prayer is talking to God, crying out to him to deliver on his promises to us. And it is the way we ask him to satisfy our desires—desires that are shaped as we read the Bible. We also express gratitude and praise to God in prayer (Eph. 1:15–16; 3:20–21). In Matthew 6:9–13, Jesus taught us how to pray to God by outlining six requests (or expressed desires) to God. Can you identify each of them? In other passages, we ask God for forgiveness (1 John 1:9), for boldness to speak his Word (Eph. 6:18–20), and for the transformation of those we love (Phil. 1:9–11), including the salvation of those who do not know God (Rom. 10:1).

- What is prayer?
- What are some ways that you could improve your prayer life?

For Reflection and Discussion

Use the space below to respond to the following questions, to record your prayers to God, and/or to prepare to process this information with others.

1. In one sentence, summarize one of the most important things that you learned in this lesson about God (including his characteristics, words, and/or actions) and how you plan to respond to that truth (in your heart, words, and/or actions). "Because God _____, I will _____."
2. Why are you thankful to God for his work in and around you?
3. Name one or more of your desires that you want to bring to God in prayer (for yourself and/or for others).

Lesson Eleven: We Are Growing into the Likeness of Jesus

Overview

For all of us who are Christians, God's will is that we become "conformed to the image of his Son" (Rom. 8:29). Put simply, he wants us to be more like Jesus, not only in our words and actions but also in our character. This transformation of our character includes the way we think, what we desire, and what we value. While there are many things in life that are out of our control, our character is not. This lesson explores three related ways that Christians grow into the likeness of Jesus.

1. We look to Jesus.

> Therefore, since we also have such a large cloud of witnesses surrounding us, let us lay aside every hindrance and the sin that so easily ensnares us. Let us run with endurance the race that lies before us, keeping our eyes on Jesus, the source and perfecter of our faith. For the joy that lay before him, he endured the cross, despising the shame, and sat down at the right hand of the throne of God. For consider him who endured such hostility from sinners against himself, so that you won't grow weary and give up. (Heb. 12:1–3)

The "witnesses" of Hebrews 11 modeled the faith that we must imitate (Heb. 12:1). They personally witnessed truths about God, his Word, and his mighty works, and they shared those truths with others. As we consider their lives, the author of Hebrews encourages us to run this race of life by laying aside obstacles to our faith, particularly our sins (vv. 1, 4). We endure in this race by looking to Jesus, the one who endured the cross to bring us to God (v. 2). He is our model of endurance, but he is also the atoning sacrifice for our sins (7:27; 9:26). Jesus's race—particularly his life, death, and resurrection—is the ground under our feet (2:9–11).

- Explain and personalize this word picture: You are a Christian running in a race. From what are you running? To where? With whom? For what reasons do you run? What sins are tripping you up?
- Instead of choosing to sin, we should keep our eyes on Jesus. What does that look like in practice?

2. We pursue Christian character.

- "Therefore, put to death what belongs to your earthly nature: sexual immorality, impurity, lust, evil desire, and greed, which is idolatry. Because of these, God's wrath is coming upon the disobedient, and you once walked in these things when you were living in them. But now, put away all the following: anger, wrath, malice, slander, and filthy language from your mouth. Do not lie to one another, since you have put off the old self with its practices." (Col. 3:5–9)
- "And have put on the new self. You are being renewed in knowledge according to the image of your Creator. In Christ there is not Greek and Jew, circumcision and uncircumcision, barbarian, Scythian, slave and free; but Christ is all and in all. Therefore, as God's chosen ones, holy and dearly loved, put on compassion, kindness, humility, gentleness, and patience, bearing with one another and forgiving one another if anyone has a grievance against another. Just as the Lord has forgiven you, so you are also to forgive. Above all, put on love, which is the perfect bond of unity." (Col. 3:10–14)

As Christians, we put our sins to death, which we do (again and again) until this life is over (Col. 3:5–9). We do so by turning from them and turning to Jesus in faith. Christians will still struggle with sin, but, ultimately, such living is a way of the past. Instead of continuing in sin, we put on the character of Jesus (vv. 10–14).

- In light of Colossians 3:5–9, where do you struggle and why?
- In light of Colossians 3:10–14, where do you most want to grow?

3. We grow through our trials.

- "Consider it a great joy, my brothers and sisters, whenever you experience various trials, because you know that the testing of your faith produces endurance. And let endurance have its full effect, so that you may be mature and complete, lacking nothing." (James 1:2–4)
- "Blessed is the one who endures trials, because when he has stood the test he will receive the crown of life that God has promised to those who love him." (James 1:12)

Trials take many forms, such as relational conflicts, financial pressures, and physical challenges. Each of them tests our faith. In the midst of our trials, God calls us to choose joy. We experience joy in God himself (Ps. 32:11), in his Word (Ps. 119:16), and in his work in others' lives (Phil. 1:3–5). While trials often lead to other reactions (like sadness and frustration), we also view trials as opportunities to rejoice, precisely because God uses our trials to shape our character (James 1:2). As God tests and refines our faith through trials, we grow in endurance, which is the ability to stand strong under the burdens of this life (v. 3). As this character quality grows, it leads us to mature more fully, "lacking nothing" (v. 4). All who endure trials are blessed indeed, for God will grant them eternal life (James 1:12).

- How are you tempted to manage your trials in sinful ways? For example, are you tempted to medicate your emotional pain? How so?
- How is God shaping your character through your trials?

For Reflection and Discussion

Use the space below to respond to the following questions, to record your prayers to God, and/or to prepare to process this information with others.

1. In one sentence, summarize one of the most important things that you learned in this lesson about God (including his characteristics, words, and/or actions) and how you plan to respond to that truth (in your heart, words, and/or actions). "Because God _____, I will _____."
2. Why are you thankful to God for his work in and around you?
3. Name one or more of your desires that you want to bring to God in prayer (for yourself and/or for others).

Lesson Twelve: We Serve Those in Need

Overview

God calls us to be men and women of Christlike character wherever we are, whether in our families, churches, communities, at work, or anywhere else. In each of these contexts, our most immediate purpose is to serve others, precisely because we value those in need. For example, our children need help with their homework, our churches and missionaries need financial support, and our neighbors need to see and feel the love of Christ. Ultimately, we do all these things and more to glorify God.

1. We work diligently at our God-given responsibilities.

> For we hear that there are some among you who are idle. They are not busy but busybodies. Now we command and exhort such people by the Lord Jesus Christ to work quietly and provide for themselves. But as for you, brothers and sisters, do not grow weary in doing good. (2 Thess. 3:11–13)

From the beginning, God created humanity to work: "The LORD God took the man and placed him in the Garden of Eden to work it and watch over it" (Gen. 2:15). That call to work remains. Depending on our age and stage in life, our main responsibilities will change, whether we are working as a student, as a parent, and/or at a full-time or part-time job. But working hard at those main responsibilities is perhaps the most immediate way that we can serve others, serve society, and serve God.

Even though our life settings are different, Paul and his ministry partners serve as ideal role models in their motivations and work ethic, particularly as we do the work of ministry (2 Thess. 3:7–9). Paul taught that those who are idle busybodies should work quietly and earn their own living (vv. 11–12). He then encouraged the church to "not grow weary in doing good" (v. 13), which is excellent advice for all of us.

- Which role models do you want to imitate in these matters? What, specifically, do you appreciate about them?
- As you consider the responsibilities God has for you, what are some practical ways that you could be more faithful?

2. We give financially.

God does not need money, for he is the source, owner, and provider of all good things (Ps. 50:10–12; James 1:17). But he commands that we give financially for a variety of reasons (1 Cor. 16:2). As we obey God, he progressively aligns our hearts and minds with his own. What follows are various characteristics of Christian giving taken from 2 Corinthians 8–9.

Christian giving is:

- generous, not stingy (2 Cor. 8:2),
- voluntary, not enforced (2 Cor. 8:3),
- enthusiastic, not grudging (2 Cor. 8:4),
- sensible, not reckless (2 Cor. 8:12), and
- deliberate, not haphazard (2 Cor. 9:7).[8]

In the process of contributing our financial resources, several things happen. We express our desire for the advancement of God's work. We cherish our local churches and how God is using them. And, ultimately, we celebrate God as the Giver of all good things, particularly the gift of Jesus (2 Cor. 8:9).

- Why should you prioritize giving to your own local church?
- Evaluate your own habits of giving. In what ways might God want you to change your habits of giving (particularly to your local church)?

---

[8] Taken from Harris, *The Second Epistle to the Corinthians*, 124.

3. We use our spiritual gifts.

> Now as we have many parts in one body, and all the parts do not have the same function, in the same way we who are many are one body in Christ and individually members of one another. According to the grace given to us, we have different gifts: If prophecy, use it according to the proportion of one's faith; if service, use it in service; if teaching, in teaching; if exhorting, in exhortation; giving, with generosity; leading, with diligence; showing mercy, with cheerfulness. (Rom. 12:4–8)

The human body consists of different parts, and those parts have different functions (Rom. 12:4). In a like manner, the one body of Christ consists of different individuals with different contributions to make, and we are members of one another (v. 5). It is natural, then, to ask how each of us can contribute to the larger body of Christ. One answer is that we use our spiritual gifts, which are Spirit-empowered abilities that God gives us for the strengthening of the church. The gifts include faith, service, teaching, and exhorting others to grow in the faith (vv. 6–8). For each of us, we exercise the gift in a way that is fitting to the gift and helpful for others—all to the glory of God (1 Pet. 4:10–11).

- How have you benefited from the spiritual gifts of others?
- What specific steps might you take to identify, develop, and use your spiritual gifts for the benefit of others and the glory of God?

For Reflection and Discussion

Use the space below to respond to the following questions, to record your prayers to God, and/or to prepare to process this information with others.

1. In one sentence, summarize one of the most important things that you learned in this lesson about God (including his characteristics, words, and/or actions) and how you plan to respond to that truth (in your heart, words, and/or actions). "Because God _____, I will _____."
2. Why are you thankful to God for his work in and around you?
3. Name one or more of your desires that you want to bring to God in prayer (for yourself and/or for others).

Lesson Thirteen: We Help Non-Christians to Know God

Overview

God calls us to help others whether they are Christians or not—within our families, in our communities, and at work. But when we discover that someone is not a Christian, perhaps the most profound way to express love is to share how he or she can enter a personal relationship with God through Jesus Christ. If the situation were reversed, isn't that what you would want someone to do for you (to help you know God)? Christians and non-Christians alike need to learn more about God the Father, reflect on the nature and consequences of their sins, and hear the gospel message.

1. We invite others to know God the Father.

> Everything is from God [the Father], who has reconciled us to himself through Christ and [God the Father] has given us the ministry of reconciliation. That is, in Christ, God [the Father] was reconciling the world to himself, not counting their trespasses against them, and he [God the Father] has committed the message of reconciliation to us. Therefore, we are ambassadors for Christ, since God [the Father] is making his appeal through us. We plead on Christ's behalf: "Be reconciled to God [the Father]." He [God the Father] made the one who did not know sin [Jesus] to be sin for us, so that in him [Jesus] we might become the righteousness of God [the Father]. (2 Cor. 5:18–21)

Before we became Christians (assuming you have done so), our relationship to God was broken, alienated, and unreconciled. But because we are now reconciled to God, we embrace the privilege and responsibility of introducing others to God the Father through the person and work of Jesus Christ.

- What does it mean if two people become reconciled? What, then, does it mean that we have a ministry of reconciliation (between God and others)?
- What does it mean to be an ambassador? What obstacles stand in the way of you becoming a more effective ambassador for Jesus Christ? How can you overcome those obstacles?

2. We proclaim and explain the gospel.

- "For I passed on to you as most important what I also received: that Christ died for our sins according to the Scriptures, that he was buried, that he was raised on the third day according to the Scriptures." (1 Cor. 15:3–4)
- "For I am not ashamed of the gospel, because it is the power of God for salvation to everyone who believes, first to the Jew, and also to the Greek." (Rom. 1:16)

The gospel is the good news that Jesus died and rose from the dead to create the only way to God (1 Cor. 15:3–4). Any "gospel" that minimizes or ignores Jesus's death and resurrection (claiming, for example, that we are saved through good works) is not the gospel (Gal. 1:1–10). The gospel is power from God that accomplishes the salvation of his people (Rom. 1:16). We receive the gospel (Gal. 1:9), are strengthened by it (Rom. 16:25), proclaim it to others (Eph. 6:19), and suffer for it (2 Tim. 1:8). This gospel calls for a response. Repentance and trust are not the gospel, but they are the necessary and most appropriate responses to the gospel.

- What is the gospel? How does the gospel make it possible to come to God?
- What are some of the most appropriate responses to the gospel? How does the gospel make practical differences in your life?

3. We call people to repent and trust in Jesus.

> He told them, "These are my words that I spoke to you while I was still with you—that everything written about me in the Law of Moses, the Prophets, and the Psalms must be fulfilled." Then he opened their minds to understand the Scriptures. He also said to them, "This is what is written: The Messiah will suffer and rise from the dead the third day, and repentance for forgiveness of sins will be proclaimed in his name to all the nations, beginning at Jerusalem. You are witnesses of these things. And look, I am sending you what my Father promised. As for you, stay in the city until you are empowered from on high." (Luke 24:44–49)

If people lack knowledge about God the Father, we start there, explaining how he is the Creator, Life Giver, and Ruler over all people (Acts 14:15–17; 17:24–31). We also explain the nature of sin and its consequences (Rom. 1:25; 3:23; 6:23). We then explain that Jesus died and rose from the dead (Luke 24:44–46). But we must also call people to turn from their sins and to receive forgiveness through faith in Jesus Christ (Luke 24:47; Acts 20:21). Only then will people understand the choice that stands before them. It is impossible for us to witness to Jesus without the power and guidance of the Holy Spirit, who God graciously gives to all Christians (Luke 24:48–49; Acts 1:8; 2:38).

- What does it mean to be a witness *to* Jesus and a witness *for* Jesus?
- How would you explain the concepts of *repentance* and *forgiveness* to others? What is the difference between a merely intellectual faith and one that leads to salvation?

For Reflection and Discussion

Use the space below to respond to the following questions, to record your prayers to God, and/or to prepare to process this information with others.

1. In one sentence, summarize one of the most important things that you learned in this lesson about God (including his characteristics, words, and/or actions) and how you plan to respond to that truth (in your heart, words, and/or actions). "Because God _____, I will _____."
2. Why are you thankful to God for his work in and around you?
3. Name one or more of your desires that you want to bring to God in prayer (for yourself and/or for others).

Lesson Fourteen: We Share the Good News with Others

Overview

This lesson allows us to consider more specifically how we can help introduce others to God through Jesus Christ—sharing with them, in particular, the good news that Jesus died and rose from the dead. We will study two Scripture passages (from Matthew 10 and Luke 10) where Jesus sent out his followers. Not every part of these passages is directly applicable to our lives. For example, after his resurrection, Jesus called his followers to go and make disciples not only of the Jews but *of all nations* (Matt. 10:5–6; 28:18–20; Acts 1:8). But there is still much we can learn about taking the message about Jesus into the world.

Jesus Sends Out the Twelve

⁵ Jesus sent out these twelve after giving them instructions: "Don't take the road that leads to the Gentiles, and don't enter any Samaritan town. ⁶ Instead, go to the lost sheep of the house of Israel. ⁷ As you go, proclaim, 'The kingdom of heaven has come near.' ⁸ Heal the sick, raise the dead, cleanse those with leprosy, drive out demons. Freely you received, freely give. ⁹ Don't acquire gold, silver, or copper for your money-belts. ¹⁰ Don't take a traveling bag for the road, or an extra shirt, sandals, or a staff, for the worker is worthy of his food. ¹¹ When you enter any town or village, find out who is worthy, and stay there until you leave. ¹² Greet a household when you enter it, ¹³ and if the household is worthy, let your peace be on it; but if it is unworthy, let your peace return to you. ¹⁴ If anyone does not welcome you or listen to your words, shake the dust off your feet when you leave that house or town. ¹⁵ Truly I tell you, it will be more tolerable on the day of judgment for the land of Sodom and Gomorrah than for that town." (Matt. 10:5–15)

> Briefly summarize each verse in this passage, which will help you reflect on how these verses apply to your life.

v. 5: [Example: Jesus sent out his disciples, but he instructed them not to go to the Gentiles (non-Jews) or to enter any Samaritan town.]

v. 6:

v. 7:

v. 8:

v. 9:

v. 10:

v. 11:

v. 12:

v. 13:

v. 14:

v. 15:

Jesus Sends Out the Seventy-Two

¹ After this, the Lord appointed seventy-two others, and he sent them ahead of him in pairs to every town and place where he himself was about to go. ² He told them, "The harvest is abundant, but the workers are few. Therefore, pray to the Lord of the harvest to send out workers into his harvest. ³ Now go; I'm sending you out like lambs among wolves. ⁴ Don't carry a money-bag, traveling bag, or sandals; don't greet anyone along the road. ⁵ Whatever house you enter, first say, 'Peace to this household.' ⁶ If a person of peace is there, your peace will rest on him; but if not, it will return to you. ⁷ Remain in the same house, eating and drinking what they offer, for the worker is worthy of his wages. Don't move from house to house. ⁸ When you enter any town, and they welcome you, eat the things set before you. ⁹ Heal the sick who are there, and tell them, 'The kingdom of God has come near you.' ¹⁰ When you enter any town, and they don't welcome you, go out into its streets and say, ¹¹ 'We are wiping off even the dust of your town that clings to our feet as a witness against you. Know this for certain: The kingdom of God has come near.' ¹² I tell you, on that day it will be more tolerable for Sodom than for that town." (Luke 10:1–12)

> Briefly summarize each verse in this passage, which will help you reflect on how these verses apply to your life.

v. 1:

v. 2:

v. 3:

v. 4:

v. 5:

v. 6:

v. 7:

v. 8:

v. 9:

v. 10:

v. 11:

v. 12:

Jesus Sends Us

Use these two pages to create a strategy for helping your non-Christian family members, friends, and neighbors to know God through Jesus Christ.

1. Learn from Scripture

> Regarding your summary statements from the previous two pages, what truths apply to you as Jesus sends you?

"With God's help, I will…"

2. Seek Out a Ministry Partner

A ministry partner will help you as you pray together, fast together, and lead a study together. Therefore, pray for guidance from God, and then invite one or more other Christians to help you in reaching those within your sphere of influence.

> - What qualities are you looking for in a ministry partner?
> - Which Christians might you ask to join you in this process (for example, to reach those in your neighborhood)?

3. Fast and Pray

When we skip one or more meals for the purposes of reading God's Word and prayer, we communicate that God, his Word, and his will are more important than food. Fasting and prayer also prepare us to reach out to our non-Christian family members, friends, neighbors, and/or coworkers.

- How and when do you plan to fast and pray?[9]
- For whom will you pray regularly? List their names below.

4. Go and Make Disciples

What does it look like *to go to others*? For starters: we walk regularly in our neighborhoods, pray with and for those we meet, offer to help them in concrete ways, and invite them to share a meal with us. In time, we ask, "Would you be willing to study the Bible with me to discover what it says about how to know God and do his will?"

- What specific strategies might you use to connect more regularly with the non-Christians around you?
- Who might God want you to invite to study God's Word with you (using this book)?

---

[9] See ChristianGathering.org/how-to-combine-prayer-and-fasting for more information.

Lesson Fifteen: We Help Christians to Know God Better

Overview

When we meet people who are not Christians, one of the most loving things we can do is explain how they can know God through Jesus Christ. But when we meet people who are Christians, one of the most loving things we can do is to help them to know God better. And we encourage them to love and obey Jesus Christ in every area of their lives. This lesson emphasizes how we can encourage fellow Christians accordingly.

1. We make followers of Jesus Christ.

 > Jesus came near and said to them, "All authority has been given to me in heaven and on earth. Go, therefore, and make disciples of all nations, baptizing them in the name of the Father and of the Son and of the Holy Spirit, teaching them to observe everything I have commanded you. And remember, I am with you always, to the end of the age." (Matt. 28:18–20)

Faithfulness to Jesus requires that we submit to his God-given authority (Matt. 28:18). The main phrase in this passage is Jesus's commandment for us to "make disciples" (v. 19). This includes both evangelizing non-Christians and discipling Christians to follow Jesus. We make disciples "of all nations" because the scope of our task extends to the end of the earth. This requires that we (1) go to people and to places (as opposed to waiting passively for people to come to us), (2) baptize new believers in the one name of the triune God (Father, Son, and Holy Spirit), and (3) teach them to obey all that Jesus commanded (which requires active involvement in their lives). Taken together, that is Jesus's Great Commission. Jesus's presence guides, empowers, and emboldens us as we seek to make disciples (v. 20). And this task would be impossible without him.

- What is the Great Commission? What obstacles stand in the way of you adopting the Great Commission as your own mission in life?
- What are several ways you can contribute to our great task?

2. We direct others to God's Word.

- "But as for you, continue in what you have learned and firmly believed. You know those who taught you, and you know that from infancy you have known the sacred Scriptures, which are able to give you wisdom for salvation through faith in Christ Jesus." (2 Tim. 3:14–15)
- "All Scripture is inspired by God and is profitable for teaching, for rebuking, for correcting, for training in righteousness, so that the man of God may be complete, equipped for every good work." (2 Tim. 3:16–17)
- "I solemnly charge you before God and Christ Jesus, who is going to judge the living and the dead, and because of his appearing and his kingdom: Preach the word; be ready in season and out of season; rebuke, correct, and encourage with great patience and teaching." (2 Tim. 4:1–2)

One of the most concrete ways that we make disciples of Jesus is by directing people to God's Word. We encourage them to submit to the Word of God (2 Tim. 3:14–15), to see its divine origin and usefulness (vv. 16–17), and to minister to others with it (2 Tim. 4:1–2). The apostle Paul said, "I have fought the good fight, I have finished the race, I have kept the faith" (2 Tim. 4:7). In his life and ours, Word-centeredness is what carries us along until we cross the finish line. Word-centeredness is also what we pass along to others, so they, too, will finish the race.

> - Why must your ministry to others be grounded in God's Word?
> - How can you encourage others to be more Word-centered?

3. We teach others to pray.

> "Therefore, you should pray like this: 'Our Father in heaven, your name be honored as holy. Your kingdom come. Your will be done on earth as it is in heaven. Give us today our daily bread. And forgive us our debts, as we also have forgiven our debtors. And do not bring us into temptation [or testing], but deliver us from the evil one.'" (Matt. 6:9–13)

In this passage, Jesus outlines how we should pray and, therefore, how we should teach others to pray. We pray:

- for God to cause others to honor his name (v. 9).
- for God's kingdom to come and his will to be done (v. 10).
- for God to supply our daily needs (v. 11).
- for God to forgive our sins (v. 12).
- for God to keep us from severe trials that test our faith (v. 13).
- for God to deliver us from the evil one, Satan (v. 13).

We learn and teach others to pray by studying Scripture's teachings and by praying together. Over time, the desires of our hearts align more and more with God's revealed will in Scripture (John 14:13).

- What desires do you want to bring to God?
- What advice would you give to others who are learning how to pray for the first time?

For Reflection and Discussion

Use the space below to respond to the following questions, to record your prayers to God, and/or to prepare to process this information with others.

1. In one sentence, summarize one of the most important things that you learned in this lesson about God (including his characteristics, words, and/or actions) and how you plan to respond to that truth (in your heart, words, and/or actions). "Because God _____, I will _____."
2. Why are you thankful to God for his work in and around you?
3. Name one or more of your desires that you want to bring to God in prayer (for yourself and/or for others).

Lesson Sixteen: We Center Our Lives on God

Overview

To this point, we have explored what it means to embrace our new identity in Christ, pursue Christlike character, serve others, and make disciples as our central mission in life. But the *ultimate goal* of our lives is not any of these. The ultimate, unifying goal of the Christian life is to be God-centered in all that we do—trusting, loving, and worshiping God above all.

1. We trust in God.

- "For you are saved by grace through faith, and this is not from yourselves; it is God's gift—not from works, so that no one can boast." (Eph. 2:8–9)
- "Trust in the LORD with all your heart, and do not rely on your own understanding; in all your ways know him, and he will make your paths straight." (Prov. 3:5–6)

God is both willing and able to follow through on his promises. Therefore, he is worthy of our trust. When we trust God, we express confidence in him as a person, in his attributes, in his promises, and in his actions. In addition to turning from our sins, trust is the means by which we enter a relationship with God (Rom. 4:5; Gal. 2:16; Eph. 2:8–9). We trust in God and in Jesus in every area of our lives (Prov. 3:5–6; Gal. 2:20), not only for our salvation. By faith, we fight for godly character and battle against sins such as anxiety (Matt. 6:25, 30), pride (Jer. 9:23), and lust (Matt. 5:27–30). By faith we serve God in concrete acts of obedience (Heb. 11). And by faith, we endure suffering and resist temptation until the end of our lives (Rev. 14:12).

- What makes God worthy of your trust? In other words, what makes him so reliable in your life as compared to other people and things?
- In what areas of your life do you need to trust God more fully? How would doing so translate into changed behavior?

2. We love God.

- "[Jesus] said to him, 'Love the Lord your God with all your heart, with all your soul, and with all your mind.'" (Matt. 22:37)
- "The one who has my commands and keeps them is the one who loves me. And the one who loves me will be loved by my Father. I also will love him and will reveal myself to him." (John 14:21)

Loving God the Father is the greatest commandment (Matt. 22:37–38), but it is no less true that we love Jesus. We express our love for Jesus primarily through our obedience to him (John 14:21; 15:9–10). While the Holy Spirit is certainly worthy of our love, one of his primary ministries is to cultivate our love for God the Father, for Jesus, and for others. The Holy Spirit not only fills our hearts with love (Rom. 5:5) but he also cultivates our expressions of love (Gal. 5:22). In addition to loving God, we love our neighbors as ourselves (Matt. 22:39). In the process, we express a particular devotion for those in the family of God, who are our brothers and sisters in Christ (Matt. 25:40; 1 John 3:14).

- How can you express your love for God in concrete ways?
- How can you express your love for others in concrete ways?

3. We worship God.

- "I heard every creature in heaven, on earth, under the earth, on the sea, and everything in them say, Blessing and honor and glory and power be to the one seated on the throne, and to the Lamb, forever and ever!" (Rev. 5:13)
- "And don't get drunk with wine, which leads to reckless living, but be filled by the Spirit: speaking to one another in psalms, hymns, and spiritual songs, singing and making music with your heart to the Lord." (Eph. 5:18–19)
- "In view of the mercies of God, I urge you to present your bodies as a living sacrifice, holy and pleasing to God; this is your true worship." (Rom. 12:1)

All people worship. Broadly defined, worship is the way we experience and express what we value most. Christians believe that the God of the Bible is the one true God who is worthy of our ultimate attention and affection. That is why Christians worship God and fight against the temptation to overvalue other people and things (Rom. 1:25). We worship by ascribing ultimate worth to God (Rev. 5:13). We worship by expressing God's worth through words (Eph. 5:18–19). And we worship by expressing God's worth in action (Rom. 12:1).

- How do you, at times, value people and things more than God?
- What are practical ways you can express that you value God more than anything else?

For Reflection and Discussion

Use the space below to respond to the following questions, to record your prayers to God, and/or to prepare to process this information with others.

1. In one sentence, summarize one of the most important things that you learned in this lesson about God (including his characteristics, words, and/or actions) and how you plan to respond to that truth (in your heart, words, and/or actions). "Because God _____, I will _____."
2. Why are you thankful to God for his work in and around you?
3. Name one or more of your desires that you want to bring to God in prayer (for yourself and/or for others).

Next Steps

1. Meet one-on-one with the person who invited you to read this book. Discuss and pray about (a) the five steps for starting a study that are listed in the introduction to this book and (b) additional strategies for starting a study that you identified in lesson fourteen.

2. Follow through on your strategies for reaching those you love with the message of Jesus Christ. For example, invite your family members, friends, and neighbors to share a meal with you on a regular basis, and then study this book together. By the grace of God, you will then help them to reach those within their spheres of influence for the eternal good of others and the glory of God.

3. See ChristianGathering.org for more information about how to grow in your faith and lead within your church.

References

Crossway. *ESV Study Bible (ESVSB)*. Wheaton, IL: Crossway, 2008.

Grudem, Wayne. *Systematic Theology: An Introduction to Biblical Doctrine* (2nd ed.). Grand Rapids, MI: Zondervan, 2020.

Harris, Murray. *The Second Epistle to the Corinthians: A Commentary on the Greek Text*. Grand Rapids, MI: Eerdmans, 2005.

Holman Bible Publishers. *CSB Study Bible (CSBSB)*. Nashville, TN: Holman Bible Publishers, 2017.

Whitney, Donald. *Spiritual Disciplines for the Christian Life*. Colorado Springs, CO: NavPress, 2014.

Acknowledgments

I am grateful for:

- Christi McGuire, for her professionalism and support as my editor.
- Hannah Vogltanz, for her great skill and encouragement as my proofreader.
- Renée Yearwood, for her internal and external design work.

Printed in the USA
CPSIA information can be obtained
at www.ICGtesting.com
JSHW081415061223
52997JS00001B/3

9 781734 480047